Bristol Railways
1978 - 1990

Colin Scott-Morton
from the Arthur Turner collection

© Images and design Transport Treasury 2022 Text Colin Scott-Morton

ISBN 978-1-913893-25-5

First published in 2022 by Transport Treasury Publishing Limited. 16 Highworth Close, High Wycombe, HP13 7PJ

Totem Publishing an imprint of Transport Treasury Publishing.

www.ttpublishing.co.uk

Printed in Tarxien, Malta By Gutenberg Press Ltd.

'*Bristol Railways 1978 - 1990*' is one of a series of books on specialist transport subjects published in strictly limited numbers and produced under the Totem Publishing imprint using material only available at The Transport Treasury.

Front Cover: HST sets began operating some of the inter-regional services from 1982, and on 5th June that year power car 43168 leads a Plymouth to Leeds service through Parson Street station. Reflecting different levels of demand on the cross-country routes, the sets allocated to these services had only a single first-class coach - as seen here behind the power car - then a catering vehicle and five second-class coaches. Parson Street station is located towards the western end of the Bristol conurbation, in the suburb of Bedminster. Just west of the station is the junction with the branch line to Portishead. Passenger services ceased on the branch in 1964, and freight in 1981, but it was reopened as far as Pill to serve a new spur to Portbury docks in 2002, and plans are now well advanced for the proposed restoration of passenger services to Portishead in 2024.

Frontispiece: Among its various outcomes, the British Railways Modernisation Plan of 1955 saw the introduction of large numbers of diesel multiple-units (DMU) to replace steam traction, largely on secondary and branch services. These were built to a variety of different designs, both by BR's own workshops and private contractors, with over 4,000 vehicles entering service between 1955 and 1963. The Class 119 sets were produced by the Gloucester Railway Carriage and Wagon Co Ltd from 1958, and worked widely across the Western Region. In this view on 17th May 1978, unit B581 pauses at Sea Mills, on the line from Severn Beach and Avonmouth to Bristol. The abandoned down platform in the foreground was taken out of use when much of the line was singled in 1970. *AT526*

Back cover: The Tonbridge to Hastings line on the Southern Region had a number of tunnels with very restricted clearances, which could only be traversed by rolling stock built to a special loading gauge. Passenger services were operated by narrow-bodied diesel multiple-units, but the line also generated some freight traffic in the form of gypsum trains from the mines near Mountfield. To operate these, the final twelve Class 33 locomotives - designated Class 33/2 - were built to the Hastings line loading gauge, with bodies 8 feet 8 inches wide rather than 9 feet 3 inches on the standard machines. This also earned them the nickname of 'Slim Jims' among enthusiasts. On 10th July 1983, one of the sub-class - 33 209 - stands at Temple Meads with a Cardiff to Portsmouth service. The narrow profile is most obvious from the bodyside being flush with the solebar, rather than extending beyond it.

Introduction

In addition to its status as a major city and port, Bristol has long been a significant centre on the railway network. Originally served by both the Great Western and Midland railways and their various constituent companies, in British Rail days it remained an important 'hub', playing host to services from London to South Wales, Devon and Cornwall, the North and the Midlands to the South West, and from the South Coast to South Wales. With a population of around half a million, the city and its surroundings also generated significant traffic in its own right. Freight flows through the area were considerable as well, with bulk movements of aggregates, coal and petroleum products, together with wagonload services operated under the 'Speedlink' brand from the late 1970s. There were also numerous trip workings between the various local freight facilities, including Bristol East and West depots, Kingsland Road, Barton Hill, Avonside Wharf and Stoke Gifford yard.

The city's main station, Temple Meads, is located on Brunel's original 1840s route from London to Exeter. Heading north from the junctions just east of Temple Meads is the 1863 line to New Passage, built originally to connect with ferries to South Wales, and subsequently providing access to the Severn Tunnel once this opened in 1886. The next important link was the 1903 'cut-off' from Wootton Bassett which joined the line to the tunnel at Patchway, avoiding Temple Meads and shortening the distance between London and South Wales by 10 miles. Bristol Parkway station, opened in 1972, is located at the western end of this line, with Stoke Gifford and Filton junctions providing routes both towards the tunnel and Temple Meads. A few miles east, the former Midland Railway line from Gloucester joins at Westerleigh junction, and this route has been used by inter-regional services from the Midlands and the North since 1970, when the MR direct line to Temple Meads was closed. There are also a handful of branch lines in the area; from Parson Street junction to Portishead, mothballed since 1981; from Stoke Gifford to Hallen Marsh, used for freight only since 1964, and from Narroways Hill junction to Severn Beach, still very much in use for passengers and some freight.

The images that follow were taken in and around Bristol between 1978 and 1990, a period of transition on the railway network and one full of interest for the observer. The Western Region's unique fleet of diesel-hydraulic locomotives had all left the scene by this time, with the last of them - the Class 52 'Westerns' - seeing final withdrawal in 1977. However, there was new equipment in evidence, in the form of the recently introduced High Speed Train

sets and Class 56 locomotives and, a few years later, the second generation diesel multiple-units of the 'Sprinter' family. Perhaps what was most striking though, while selecting these images, was just how much variety there was to be seen during those twelve years, and how much has changed since. No fewer than 26 different classes of locomotive and multiple-unit are represented, of which 17 are no longer to be seen on the National network, although many have found their way into preservation. Unfitted freight trains are a thing of the past, as are the numerous relief services that ran during summer weekends to cater for crowds to and from the West Country. Many locations have changed out of all recognition, with the few manual signal boxes and semaphore signals that remained at the time now replaced by modern technology, and depots and freight facilities closed or rationalised. On the positive side, there are new and reopened stations at Filton Abbey Wood and Yate, reinstatement of four tracks between Filton and Bristol (reversing a rationalisation depicted in the following pages), and proposals for the restoration of passenger services to Portishead, Henbury, and Charfield.

The period covered also saw some developing variety in liveries. Initially, this comprised various adjustments made by individual depots to the all-encompassing BR blue - especially on refurbished diesel multiple-units - together with branding applied by some passenger transport executives. The subsequent reorganisation of British Rail - moving away from a regional structure to one based on business sectors focused on specific markets - brought further change still, with striking new schemes dispensing with the old BR colours altogether. InterCity and Regional Railways were the major passenger operators in the area, and their liveries can be seen in some of the later images, while the colourful stripes of Network SouthEast are also evident on the sector's locomotives which found their way this far west. The various iterations of the Railfreight colours also make appearances, from the initial sector-wide plain grey, to the later two-tone scheme with sub-sector logos. The process was to continue and accelerate during the following decade, with franchising bringing many new operators and brands, but that is outside the scope of this volume.

I would like to thank all of those at Transport Treasury for their help and efforts in sourcing the images from which this selection was made, and I hope that readers find as much pleasure in browsing through it, as I have had putting it together.

Colin Scott-Morton, October 2022

The diesel-powered High Speed Train (HST) was developed during the early 1970s, initially intended as a 'stopgap' until the proposed Advanced Passenger Train (APT) was ready for service. Development of the latter was proving to be protracted, and in the meantime the HST - which could operate at speeds of up to 125 mph on existing lines - would allow journey time improvements in the face of competition from an expanding motorway network. After extensive trial running with the Class 252 prototype set, Class 253 production sets entered service on the Western Region from 1976. On 18th May 1978, set 253 011 passes Yatton, once the junction for the Clevedon and Cheddar Valley lines, with a service from Paddington to Taunton. *AT530*

The Modernisation Plan DMU fleets included a number of single cars, intended for routes where traffic levels were very light. In 1960, the Pressed Steel Company built 16 Class 121 single cars for the Western Region at its factory in Linwood, Scotland. These seated 65 passengers in a high density, two-plus-three layout, with doors to each seating bay. There were driving cabs at each end, with accommodation for the guard and luggage behind one of these. Car number W55032, also carrying set number B132, stands at Stapleton Road station on 27th May 1978. The particular working is not recorded, but is probably a service from Avonmouth or Severn Beach. *AT559*

Bridgwater is the setting for this view of Class 50 locomotive 50 026, *Indomitable,* **working a service from Paddington to the West Country on 17th June 1978. The Class 50s were built by English Electric from 1967, to meet a requirement for a mixed traffic locomotive in the type 4 bracket (2,000-2,750 hp) with 100 mph capability. They were initially allocated to the London Midland Region, and were deployed on the West Coast main line, hauling freight and Anglo-Scottish passenger services over the non-electrified sections north of Crewe. These duties reduced as electrification was extended towards Glasgow during the early 1970s, and the 50s moved to the Western Region where they replaced the Class 52 diesel-hydraulic machines.** *AT629*

The largest locomotive fleet in the type 3 bracket (1,500-1,750 hp) was the Class 37, with 309 examples turned out by English Electric from 1960. Powered by an English Electric 12CSVT 12-cylinder engine rated at 1,750 hp, they were also among the most reliable of all the diesel types, and found work widely on freight and passenger services across the BR network. On 25th July 1978, 37 190 leads a special working towards Severn Beach, passing the faded grandeur of Clifton Down station. Opened in 1874, initially as the terminus of the Clifton Extension Railway, it originally boasted generous canopies covering both platforms together with a substantial booking office and waiting rooms in the building on the left. By the date of this photograph, its status had long been reduced to that of an unstaffed halt. *AT679*

The first 119 Class 37 locomotives were built with end gangway doors, and split headcode panels displaying two characters on either side. This feature was abandoned on later builds, replaced by a plain front end with standard four-character headcode panel, subsequently converted to marker lights during the mid-1970s once trains were no longer required to carry reporting numbers. 37 183 displays the latter treatment as it heads a Bristol-bound special working through Shirehampton on the Severn Beach branch on 23rd August 1978. This is the first station east of Avonmouth, and now has just a single platform, although at the date of the photograph there was still a siding serving a small oil terminal, accessed by the points in the foreground. *AT855*

Together with their very similar sisters - Classes 44 and 45, with which they shared the collective name 'Peaks' - the Class 46s formed part of a total build of 193 locomotives turned out by BR's Derby works between 1958 and 1963. Weighing 138 tonnes and mounted on four-axle bogies with a 1Co-Co1 wheel arrangement, they were rated at 2,500 hp and had a maximum speed of 90 mph. The inter-regional services between the south-west and the north-east/north-west had long been a regular duty for the Class, with members regularly venturing as far west as Penzance once the Western Region's diesel hydraulics were withdrawn. On 31st August 1978, 46 032 has charge of one such working, from Taunton to Manchester, captured by the camera at Weston-super-Mare. *AT874*

From the mid-1950s onwards, provision was made for travellers and their cars to reach far-flung destinations by rail without the inconvenience of a long road journey, with the brand name 'Motorail' later applied to such services. Passengers travelled in ordinary coaches, while their cars were conveyed on a variety of specialised vehicles as part of the same train. The network was extensive, with extremities at Dover, Penzance, Fort William and Inverness, although routes and destinations served varied considerably over the years. By the mid-1990s, expansion of the motorway network had significantly reduced journey times by road and this, combined with the privatisation of the railway network, led to the demise of these services. On 3rd September 1978, Class 50 locomotive 50 050, *Fearless*, leads a westbound Motorail working away from Bristol Temple Meads. *AT883*

One can almost feel the cold in this view, as the exhaust from Class 118 unit B467 streams out into the frosty air on 6th January 1979. Fifteen three-coach Class 118 units were built by the Birmingham Railway Carriage and Wagon Company from 1960. The driving vehicles were both second-class, with high density two-plus-three seating; one had guard's and luggage accommodation at the inner end. The unpowered centre vehicle was a composite, with first- and second-class saloons separated by two central toilets. The particular working depicted here is not recorded, but the train is heading west past Victoria Park on the line from Bristol Temple Meads towards Bridgwater. *AT1066*

The 1,550 hp Class 33 locomotives were built by the Birmingham Railway Carriage and Wagon Company at its Smethwick works from 1960. They were a development of the company's earlier Class 26 machine, but the adoption of electric train heating alone allowed the elimination of the steam heating boiler, freeing up space for an eight-cylinder Sulzer 8DLA28B diesel engine. Although ordered specifically for the Southern Region, they were regular performers on Western lines on both internal and inter-regional services. On 12th May 1979, 33 007 heads a special working north past Narroways Hill Junction, between Bristol Temple Meads and Filton. The train appears to be formed largely of Mark 1 coaches, with the exception of a Mark 2A corridor first behind the locomotive. *AT1391*

On 26th June 1979 a mixed formation of freight vehicles - probably unfitted given the brake van at the rear - descends Filton Bank at Lockleaze behind locomotive 25 124. The Class 25s were the most numerous in the type 2 bracket (1,000-1,475 hp), some 327 locomotives entering service between 1961 and 1967. A higher powered development of the earlier Class 24, manufacture was shared between BR's Darlington and Derby works, and the private contractor Beyer Peacock. Initial allocations were to the Eastern, North Eastern, and London Midland regions, but a number of the class moved to the Western Region following the first withdrawals of diesel-hydraulic locomotives in the early 1970s, and were deployed on freight and secondary passenger services. AT1513

A Travelling Post Office (TPO) working heads north past Lockleaze behind Class 31 locomotive 31 128 on 27th June 1979. Mail was first transported by train in 1830, and by 1838 railway companies were legally obliged to carry it. The operation expanded rapidly thereafter, with purpose-built vehicles providing sorting facilities on board, and lineside equipment allowing mail bags to be picked up and set down on the move. However, the introduction of mechanised sorting systems and a gradual move to road and air transport during the 1990s saw the services decline, and the last regular TPO ran in January 2004.
An interesting feature of the TPO service was the provision of post boxes in the vehicle sides, allowing passengers to post letters from station platforms. These can just be seen in the centres of the first, second and fourth vehicles. *AT1518*

Class 08 shunter 08 825 trundles through Temple Meads with HST power car W43055 on 1st July 1979. The circumstances are not recorded, but the power car had probably been detached from - or was about to be attached to - a full set as part of maintenance operations. The Class 08 was by far the most numerous shunter operated by BR, with 996 locomotives entering service between 1953 and 1962. They were built by BR's workshops at Crewe, Darlington, Derby, Doncaster, Horwich and Swindon, and were powered by a 350 hp diesel engine with electric transmission. Once a common sight at major stations and freight yards, the increased use of multiple-units for passenger services together with trainload and intermodal freight operations has significantly reduced the requirement for shunters, and they have largely disappeared from the network. *AT1522*

The type 2 Class 31 locomotives were built by Brush Traction of Loughborough between 1957 and 1962, with the whole fleet of 263 initially allocated to the Eastern Region. They had an A1A-A1A wheel arrangement, with the centre axles of their six-wheel bogies unpowered. In 1964, major problems were identified with the original Mirrlees 1,250 hp diesel engines, and they were all replaced by English Electric 12SVT units of 1,470 hp during a three-year programme. Early examples, such as 31 110 seen here, were fitted with disc train identification equipment, but the majority of the fleet carried roof-mounted four character headcode panels. On 7th July 1979, 31 110 passes the site of Ashley Hill station, north of Narroways Hill junction, with a Weymouth to Cardiff service. *AT1544*

The 'Severnsider' rail tour on 15th July 1979 took in a number of interesting lines around Bristol and South Gloucestershire, including Avonmouth, Tytherington, Gloucester Docks and Sharpness. Motive power was provided variously by shunter 08 826, Class 37, 37 270 and Class 20, 20 154. The last mentioned is seen here, attracting some lineside attention as it brings the train off the Tytherington line at Yate. Originally serving the town of Thornbury, passenger services ceased in 1944 and goods traffic in 1966, but the line remains open as far as Tytherington to serve the quarry there. Yate station has also enjoyed a change of fortunes since this photograph was taken, reopening for passenger services on 11th May 1989. *AT1611*

Class 45 locomotive 45 058 heads north past the site of Charfield station with a Plymouth to Manchester service on 24th July 1979. Other than an increase in power output from 2,300 to 2,500 hp, there was little to distinguish the 45s from the earlier Class 44s. The example seen here was one of the batch originally built with end gangway doors, sealed up by the date of this photograph, but still evident by way of the split headcode panels. Located on the line from Bristol to Gloucester, Charfield station closed to passengers in 1965, although plans for its reopening are currently under consideration. In 1928, it was the scene of a triple collision between a mail train and two goods trains, and subsequent fire, resulting in 15 fatalities. *AT1642*

No pictorial survey of this area would be complete without a view of Bath Spa station. In this shot, on 29th August 1979, Class 47 locomotive 47 339 pauses for custom with a Cardiff to Weymouth service. The 2,750 hp Class 47s were developed as BR's 'standard' type 4 locomotive and were the most numerous of all the diesel classes, with 512 machines entering service between 1962 and 1968. There were a number of sub-classes with detail differences between them. Class 47/3 - to which 47 339 belongs - were primarily intended for freight workings and had no train heating equipment. However, this was no barrier to their deployment on passenger services during the summer months, as was the case here. *AT1897*

An interesting pairing at Bristol Bath Road depot on 31st October 1979. In the foreground sits Class 03 shunter 03 121, one of 230 such locomotives built by BR's Doncaster and Swindon works between 1957 and 1962. Powered by a 204 hp Gardner 8L3 diesel engine with mechanical transmission, their low weight and short wheelbase proved especially useful in locations which precluded use of the larger Class 08. Sitting just behind is departmental locomotive TDB 968006, originally one of the 20 Class 28 machines built by Metropolitan Vickers in 1958/9. Unusual in having a Co-Bo wheel arrangement and two-stroke engines - the latter the source of many problems - they had a relatively short service life, all being withdrawn by 1968. This one example - formerly D5705 - was taken into departmental use, and when photographed was used for carriage pre-heating. It has since been preserved. *AT2011*

Class 31 locomotive 31 158 heads east through Bristol Parkway station with a train of coal hopper wagons on 31st October 1979. Bristol Parkway was opened in 1972, and was the first of many such park and ride stations across the BR network, outside urban centres but with extensive car parking and good motorway or trunk road connections. It is located close to the M4 and M32 motorways in Stoke Gifford, on the main line between Wootton Bassett and the Severn Tunnel, and the junctions east of the station provide routes north towards the tunnel, south towards Bristol Temple Meads, and west on to the freight-only Henbury loop. *AT2016*

A Paddington to Swansea HST approaches Patchway Old Tunnel on 21st August 1980, topped and tailed by power cars 43 019 and 43 018. The initial HST sets were delivered with two catering vehicles - a restaurant kitchen car (TRUK) between first- and second-class, and a buffet car (TRSB) in place of the third second-class coach from the end. This provision was soon recognised as over-generous, and the formations were altered to include a single buffet/kitchen vehicle (TRUB) between two first- and four second-class coaches, as seen here. The down line at this point was the original 1863 single track route to New Passage, on the Severn Estuary. The line was later doubled to handle the additional traffic generated by the Severn Tunnel, and the new up line was built with a gentler gradient than the original, giving rise to the different levels seen here. *AT2858*

On 21st August 1980, a train of oil tank wagons heads towards the Severn Tunnel west of Pilning station, double-headed by Class 25 locomotives 25 211/106. The particular working is not recorded, but the train was possibly returning to Stanlow refinery. The up and down loops seen here allowed freight trains to be overtaken by passenger workings, either on exit from the tunnel or before entering it. The train depicted, however, obviously had a clear path, as it is running on the down main line. *AT2862*

The Class 101 DMUs, built by Metro-Cammell, were one of the most numerous of the Modernisation Plan types, with some 620 vehicles entering service from 1956. They were variously formed into two-, three- and four-coach sets, and this variety required a number of different vehicle types. The fleet included both powered and unpowered driving vehicles - the former fitted with either AEC or Leyland six-cylinder engines rated at 150 hp - while all intermediate vehicles were unpowered. Most of the class - 562 vehicles - underwent a refurbishment programme between 1976 and 1984. Modifications included new upholstery and fluorescent lighting, together with improvements to the heating and engine silencing systems. Externally, refurbished units carried a revised livery of white with a broad blue stripe at waist level, and unit B802 is seen in these colours at Temple Meads on 25th August 1980. *AT2891*

Keynsham station, between Bristol and Bath, is the setting for Class 33 locomotive 33 047 heading east on 25th August 1980. The train is recorded as a Bristol to Portsmouth Harbour working, but curiously it is displaying two white blanks rather than the normal headcode of '89' for this service. As well as serving the town of Keynsham and the surrounding area, the station also had a siding to the Fry's chocolate factory in nearby Somerdale. This was taken out of use about a month before this photograph was taken, the factory itself eventually closing in 2011. Train services on the Cardiff-Bristol-Portsmouth route have enjoyed a variety of diesel motive power over the years, from Class 31 and Class 35 'Hymek' locomotive haulage, to various WR and SR DMUs, but the SR's Class 33s were regular performers through the 1980s. *AT2889*

Many of the Class 45 locomotives carried the names of British Army Regiments, as typified by 45 055, *Royal Corps of Transport*, seen here at Temple Meads on 13th June 1981. Like most of the class, it had benefited from the 'tidying up' of the front end and the fitting of marker lights. In its original incarnation as D84, it had sported end gangway doors and split headcode panels, no traces of which are now visible. On this summer Saturday, 45 055 had charge of a service from Leeds to Weston-super-Mare. *AT3658*

Sidelit by evening sunshine, locomotives 37 294 and 47 901 double-head a train of loaded coal hoppers eastbound through Pilning station on 27th July 1981. 47 901 was the sole member of sub-class 47/9, fitted out in 1979 as an operational test bed with equipment for the Class 58 locomotive, then under development. Pilning is the first station east of the Severn Tunnel, and now sees little use. The footbridge from which this photograph was taken was demolished in 2016 to provide clearance for overhead catenary, and the down platform abandoned. As a result, the two 'Parliamentary' trains which call each week are both eastbound workings, passengers from the Bristol direction having to travel to Severn Tunnel Junction and then backtrack. *AT3843*

On 27th July 1981, Class 47 locomotive 47 237 heads a westbound freightliner working past Pilning. The train is on the down main line - the track in the foreground is the down goods loop which starts east of the station and runs around the back of the down platform. The transport of goods by rail in standard shipping containers was one of the recommendations in the 1963 Beeching report, and the first revenue earning service operated in 1965, with the 'Freightliner' name being adopted soon afterwards. With profitability increasing, Freightliner Ltd became a standalone legal entity in 1968, albeit still wholly owned by the government. However, a need for increased infrastructure investment, specifically to allow the use of larger containers, resulted in the operation being returned to BR control in 1978, where it remained at the time of this photograph. *AT3845*

The Class 50 locomotives were all named after Royal Navy ships in 1978/9, and this view on 23rd August 1981 shows a pairing of 50 046, *Ajax*, and 50 048, *Dauntless*. They are double-heading a Penzance to Paddington train through Stapleton Road station, near the foot of Filton Bank. By this date, most of the normal scheduled services between London and Plymouth/Penzance were formed of air-conditioned Mark 2 stock or worked by HST sets. This is almost certainly one of the many relief trains that ran throughout the summer to cater for the heavy traffic to and from the West Country, given the consist of eleven Mark 1 coaches with no catering vehicle. Such workings provided gainful employment at the weekend for these Mark 1 rakes, which were deployed on London commuter services from Newbury and Oxford during the week. *AT4127*

Class 101 unit B822 pauses at Yatton with a service towards Bristol on 6th September 1981. This unit escaped the refurbishment work undertaken on most of the fleet, and retained its plain Rail Blue livery at the date of this photograph. The other indication of its unmodified state is the presence of individual rainstrips over each door - refurbished sets were fitted with a single rainstrip running the full length of the cantrail. Yatton station enjoyed a variety of services, including local workings between Taunton, Weston-super-Mare, Bristol and Bath, Inter City services to and from London, and some of the inter-regional trains between the West Country and the Midlands and North. *AT4274*

During the 1970s, BR began design work on a second generation of diesel multiple-units to replace the large fleets introduced under the Modernisation Plan. Early experiments, aimed at keeping costs as low as possible, involved mounting an adapted Leyland bus body on a four-wheel rail chassis. Five such vehicles were built for testing and evaluation purposes, and two of them - carrying departmental numbers RDB 975874 and 977020 - operated in passenger service for a period. The data and experience gained from these operations led to orders for the large fleet of 'Pacer' units of Classes 141 to 144, introduced between 1984 and 1987. On 29th October 1981, RDB 977020 pauses at Lawrence Hill with what is probably a service to Avonmouth or Severn Beach. *AT4385*

A delightful winter scene at Lockleaze on 12th December 1981, with powdery snow on the ground and low afternoon sun highlighting the main subject. Class 33 locomotive 33 010 heads north up Filton Bank with a Portsmouth to Cardiff service. This train would have run via Southampton, Romsey, Salisbury, Westbury and Bath to reach Bristol, and then reversed in Temple Meads station before gaining access to the Filton line via Bristol East and Dr Day's junctions. The 33s were equipped for electric train heating only, so despite the conditions, there is no sign of the leaking steam that was often apparent between coaches when a steam heat fitted locomotive was employed. *AT4403*

Trowbridge, between Westbury and Bradford-on-Avon, is the most easterly location in this selection. Opened in 1848 on the Wilts, Somerset and Weymouth Railway's line between Chippenham and Westbury, the route was soon taken over by the Great Western Railway, who added the link from Bradford South Junction to Bath and Bristol nine years later. This subsequently became the 'main line', that towards Chippenham being downgraded to secondary status. In spring sunshine on 14th April 1982, locomotive 33 009 slows for the scheduled call here with a Cardiff to Portsmouth working. Note that the southbound line at least (the northbound cannot be seen) was still laid with bullhead rail at this date. *AT4560*

Viewed from Victoria Park, Class 33 locomotive 33 014 eases empty coaching stock through the carriage washer to the west of Temple Meads, while an HST heads east on the up main line. The locomotive is carrying the '89' headcode associated with services between Cardiff and Portsmouth, so the stock is probably from one of those workings. In the CK corridor composite vehicle behind the locomotive, the centremost second-class compartment has an opening 'stretcher window', identifiable by its thicker frame. These were provided in response to a Ministry of Health requirement in force when the stock was built, and allowed a sick or injured patient in a stretcher to be loaded into the compartment, if this side of the vehicle was adjacent to the platform. On the other side of the coach, there was an entrance door into the corridor directly opposite this compartment. *AT4830*

Despite the introduction of HSTs in 1982, loco-haulage was still widespread on inter-regional workings. Class 45 locomotive 45 125 heads a Paignton to Glasgow service past Parson Street on Bank Holiday Saturday, 28th August 1982. HST introduction had, however, resulted in a gradual 'cascade' of newer rolling stock to other services, and with the exception of a BG full brake behind the locomotive and a catering vehicle some way back, this train is formed of air-conditioned Mark 2 coaches. At this date, the station seems to have escaped BR corporate signage - the running-in board on the up platform is still in British Railways Western Region brown. *AT4910*

An interesting view across the 'New Cut', the artificial waterway constructed in the early 1800s to divert the River Avon in connection with development of the city's Floating Harbour. The harbour was originally served by railway lines direct from Temple Meads, and from Ashton Junction on the Portishead branch. The former closed in 1964, while the latter - seen here - survived until 1987 to serve the Western Fuel Company coal concentration depot at Wapping Wharf. The particular working here on 5th March 1983 is not recorded, but Class 37 locomotive 37 254 is standing at the head of what appears to be a rake of condemned Mark 1 coaches. *AT5857*

On Sunday 12th June 1983, the 'Brunel Pullman' railtour ran from Bristol to Worcester, hauled by King Class locomotive 6000, *King George V,* as far as Hereford, and then Stanier 'Black 5' no. 5000 for the remaining leg. Diesel haulage replaced steam on the return trip, with Class 47 locomotive 47 500, *Great Western*, heading the tour back to Bristol. As the shadows lengthen in the evening sunshine, the train nears journey's end, descending Filton Bank at Lockleaze. The smartly turned-out rolling stock is the Steam Locomotive Operators Association (SLOA) Pullman train, consisting largely of ex-Eastern Region Metro-Cammell Pullman cars. Some 'spotters' can be seen on the embankment just above the second coach, presumably well inside the railway boundary! *AT6304*

Newquay was among the destinations served by the many summer extras from the Midlands and the North, and until closure of its signal box and rationalisation of the track layout in 1987, it regularly played host to locomotive-hauled trains. On Saturday 25th June 1983, Class 50 locomotive 50 012, *Benbow*, approaches Narroways Hill junction with a service to the North Cornwall resort from Manchester. Between 1980 and 1983, the entire 50 fleet underwent a refurbishment programme at Doncaster works, primarily to address increasingly poor reliability. In addition to dealing with the technical issues, Doncaster turned out the refurbished machines in this revised livery with large BR logo and numerals, wrap round yellow ends, and black window surrounds. *AT6382*

Perhaps with heavy hearts, surfers and sunseekers have to head home at the end of their holidays, and in this view on 2nd July 1983 Class 45 locomotive 45 150 heads a Newquay to Leeds service past Easton. The locomotive looks in serious need of works attention, with paintwork in poor condition, and what appears to be a large oil stain on the bodyside towards the rear. The platforms of Lawrence Hill, the first station north of Temple Meads, can just be seen beyond the underbridge. That bridge carried the Mangotsfield to Bristol section of the former Bristol and Gloucester - and later Midland - Railway over the Great Western line, until its final closure in 1970. The trackbed now forms part of the 15-mile Bristol and Bath Railway Path. *AT6408*

Class 33 Locomotive 33 056, *The Burma Star*, **poses for the camera at Bath Road depot on 3rd July 1983. This was one of the two locomotives that hauled Earl Mountbatten's funeral train from Waterloo to Romsey on 5th September 1979, the other being 33 027,** *Earl Mountbatten of Burma*. **Both locomotives were named in a ceremony at Waterloo station three days earlier, and were turned out in immaculate ex-works condition complete with white roofs, which 33 056 still retains in this view. Located near the western end of Temple Meads station, Bath Road (shed code 82A) originally handled passenger steam locomotives, but was rebuilt as a diesel depot in the early 1960s, with the capacity to service 140 diesel locomotives.** *AT6412*

A Bristol to Leeds service heads north near Narroways Hill junction on 3rd July 1983, with Class 46 locomotive 46 014 providing the motive power. A set of 'catch points' can be seen in the northbound relief line nearest the camera. These were commonplace on rising gradients in the days of unfitted freight trains, their purpose being to derail any vehicles that had broken away from the rest of the train and were running back down the slope. They comprised a set of trailing point blades, heading away from the running line, and held in the 'reverse' position by spring pressure. A train running through in the 'normal' direction forced the blades closed, with the springs opening them again once it had passed. With the widespread introduction of fully fitted freight trains catch points were progressively removed, and are now generally found only at the exits from sidings and loops. *AT6410*

The Tonbridge to Hastings line on the Southern Region had a number of tunnels with very restricted clearances, which could only be traversed by rolling stock built to a special loading gauge. Passenger services were operated by narrow-bodied diesel multiple-units, but the line also generated some freight traffic in the form of gypsum trains from the mines near Mountfield. To operate these, the final twelve Class 33 locomotives - designated Class 33/2 - were built to the Hastings line loading gauge, with bodies 8 feet 8 inches wide rather than 9 feet 3 inches on the standard machines. This also earned them the nickname of 'Slim Jims' among enthusiasts. On 10th July 1983, one of the sub-class - 33 209 - stands at Temple Meads with a Cardiff to Portsmouth service.
AT6446

The early stages of BR's reorganisation into business sectors were accompanied by a number of new liveries. One of the first was 'InterCity Executive', which was initially applied experimentally to a pair of HST sets, nominally deployed on morning and evening 'business trains' between London, Bristol and South Wales. This was a development of the scheme carried on the abortive Advanced Passenger Train (APT), comprising a light beige lower body and dark grey upper, separated by narrow red and white bands. Power car 43 126 wears the new colours as it brings up the rear of a Weston-super-Mare to Paddington service at Stapleton Road on 17th September 1983. Either the Mark 3 coaches making up the train have yet to receive the new livery, or the power cars have been swapped between sets for maintenance purposes. *AT7007*

The Class 105 units were built by Cravens of Sheffield, some 302 vehicles being turned out between 1956 and 1959 in two- and three-coach formations. The vehicles had the same body profile as BR Mark 1 coaches, and power was provided by the fairly standard AEC or Leyland six-cylinder engines rated at 150 hp. Internal arrangements were high density, with two-plus-three seating in second class, and two-plus-two in first. None of these units were ever allocated to the Western Region. The example pictured here, on 17th September 1983, carries Eastern Region numbers E50370 and E56457 with a Norwich set number - 37 - in the windscreen. It is passing Victoria Park in company with a West Midlands PTE branded Class 101 set, and is thought to be working a Saturday Birmingham to Weston-super-Mare service. *AT6995*

Not all DMUs spent their entire working lives carrying passengers. Of the twenty Class 103 sets introduced in 1957 one - vehicles 50396/56162 - was taken into departmental use by the Railway Technical Centre at Derby in 1970. Renumbered as RDB 975089/90, with the former designated 'Laboratory Coach no. 5', the unit was fitted out with instrumentation to measure ride quality, and toured the BR network taking detailed recordings. It was also loaned to the Dutch railway operator during 1976, and spent time on the London Underground network between 1984 and 1988, before finally being withdrawn in 1990. On 12th April 1984, the set heads east through Bristol Parkway. *AT7295*

A very smart Class 120 'Cross Country' DMU slows for the Bristol Parkway stop with a service bound for Temple Meads on 13th April 1984. The 120s were built by BR's Swindon works between 1958 and 1961, with 58 units going to the Western Region and seven to Scotland. Intended for longer distance routes, they had low density two-plus-two seating in second class, and two-plus-one in first, together with a small buffet counter at one end of the centre trailer vehicle. The buffets proved uneconomical over time, and catering services were withdrawn in the mid-1970s, although the facilities remained in situ. Unit C615, seen here, was initially allocated to the Scottish Region, but transferred to Cardiff in 1980. The headlight fitted between the windscreens was a feature of all Cardiff-based units used on the Central Wales line, to provide better visibility at the many ungated level crossings on the route. *AT7296*

With Bath Road depot and the old Royal Mail sorting office buildings behind, Class 117 unit B426 sets off with a westbound working from Temple Meads on 23rd April 1984. These three-coach units were built by the Pressed Steel Company in 1959, primarily for Paddington suburban services, though with some destined for the Bristol area, Devon and Cornwall. They had high density interiors with - initially - no gangways between vehicles, although these were added from the mid-1960s onwards, giving all passengers access to the toilets in the centre trailer. This view has changed significantly since the photograph was taken, with Bath Road depot closing in 1995, and the sorting office building demolished in 2019 after over twenty years of disuse. *AT7525*

Class 31 Locomotive 31 210 runs light past Ashton junction on 12th May 1984. The locomotive is coming off the mothballed Portishead branch, the lines to the left being the remains of the original route to Bristol Harbour, still open at this date as far as the Western Fuel Company coal concentration depot at Wapping Wharf. The signal box here closed in 1991 and was demolished in 1999, with the level crossing barriers now controlled from Bristol power signal box using CCTV. 31 210 first entered service in July 1960, and after 16 years on the Eastern Region was allocated to Bristol Bath Road in May 1976. It has been preserved and is currently undergoing restoration at the Dean Forest Railway. *AT7638*

Redland is a suburb to the north of Bristol city centre, and is served by a station on the branch to Avonmouth and Severn Beach. On 12th May 1984, Class 119 DMU B595 pauses for custom with a service towards Temple Meads. These sets had the same internal layout as the Swindon built Class 120s, including the small buffet in the centre trailer. However, the buffet sections in a number of units were converted to luggage space in the early 1980s, and these areas, together with the large brake vans, were indicated by prominent external signage reading 'Passenger Luggage Stowage Area'. This can be clearly seen on the first and second vehicles in this view. This feature made the units especially suitable for the Reading to Gatwick service, and a number of sets, including B595, were transferred to Reading. *AT7628*

Locomotives and multiple-units began to be fitted with high-intensity headlights from the 1980s onwards, with Class 47 an early recipient, as seen in this view of 47 101 on 13th May 1984. The locomotive is leaving the main line just west of Parson Street and venturing cautiously on to the Portishead branch, trailing a rake of Mark 1 coaches. The train is recorded as a 'special', so may have been some sort of railtour or charter, although there are no enthusiasts hanging out of the windows with cameras, behaviour which often characterised such workings! *AT7657*

Rationalisation during 1984 saw the quadruple track on Filton Bank reduced to double, with the remaining two lines slewed at various locations to increase line speeds. In this view at Lockleaze on 10th June that year, the relief lines are clearly out of use although still in situ, as Class 45 locomotive 45 114 passes on the up main line with a Penzance to Newcastle service. In a change of fortunes over thirty years later, Network Rail decided that double track would provide insufficient capacity for planned service increases, and the four-track layout has been restored, with work completed in 2019. *AT7825*

A panoramic view westwards across Bristol Parkway on 11th June 1984. The station and its extensive car parking can be clearly seen, while behind are the hangars and runway of Filton Aerodrome, notable as - among other things - the base for Concorde during its test flying programme. The line southwards towards Filton Bank and Temple Meads can just be seen at the top left of the picture, below the hangar buildings. In the foreground, Class 37 locomotives 37 274 and 37 272 wait at the head of a train of stone hopper wagons in Stoke Gifford yard, while a lone 'Presflo' cement wagon stands in the siding on the up side. This view has changed considerably over the years; a new station building has been erected adjacent to the footbridge, both platforms are now islands, giving four faces in total, and overhead catenary has been installed. *AT7826*

Tyseley depot applied an unusual variation to the standard blue/grey livery on at least two of its Class 101 units in May 1983, comprising a black wrap-round surround to the windscreens. Set TS 417 displays this treatment, together with West Midlands PTE branding, when caught by the camera in the sunshine at Weston-super-Mare on 23rd June 1984. Given that this was a Saturday, and that the sister unit further up the platform is also West Midlands based, the pair have probably worked one of the seasonal extras from Birmingham. *AT7885*

Mishaps will occur from time to time. In this view on 1st July 1984, Class 47 locomotive 47 307 has become derailed in the sidings at Bath Road depot, and waits forlornly for recovery while two railwaymen look on. 47 307 was allocated to Healey Mills depot, near Wakefield, at this date, and as a member of sub-class 47/3, lacked train heating equipment. It had probably reached Bristol on a freight working, although the use of non-heat fitted locomotives on passenger services was not unknown during the summer months. The building immediately behind the locomotive is the depot signal box, while that further back is the old Royal Mail sorting office. *AT7902*

The Class 40 locomotives were built to meet a requirement for a type 4, 2,000 hp machine to work main-line passenger trains. An initial order was placed with English Electric for 10 locomotives, and their success in service quickly led to follow-on orders totalling 199 examples, entering service from 1958 to 1962 on the Eastern, London Midland, and Scottish regions. External styling was very similar to the manufacturer's later Class 37, but the higher weight dictated the use of a 1Co-Co1 wheel arrangement. Later examples had four-character headcode displays, but the first 323 of the fleet were fitted with disc train identification equipment, as seen here on 40 079, hauling the southbound 'Devon Belle' railtour past Lawrence Hill on 16th September 1984. This tour ran from Swansea to Paignton, starting out at 07.30 and arriving back at 22.00, allowing participants around six hours in the south Devon resort. *AT8423*

In wintry conditions on 12th February 1985, a Milford Haven to Bristol service emerges from Patchway New Tunnel, hauled by Class 47 locomotive 47 627. This tunnel, exactly one mile long, is on the more gently graded up line, which is lower at this point than the original 1863 single line seen on the left. 47 627 entered service on 13th November 1965, numbered D1974 and allocated to Haymarket depot in Edinburgh. It received its first TOPS number, 47 273, in March 1974, and was renumbered 47 627 in December 1984, shortly after being transferred to the Western Region. On 9th May 1985, just under three months after this photograph was taken, it was named *City of Oxford* by Dr Frank Garside, Lord Mayor of that city. *AT8741*

A Plymouth to York service heads east through the snow from Bristol Parkway on 12th February 1985, led by power car 43 137. When the HSTs were first introduced, guards travelled in the van area at the inner end of the power car. However, engine noise was found to be excessive in these areas, and so from 1980 alternative accommodation was provided in newly built Trailer Guard Second (TGS) vehicles, effectively a Trailer Second with the end vestibule and one seating bay replaced by a guard's compartment. These vehicles were always marshalled next to the power car - which retained luggage accommodation and brake controls - and an example can be seen immediately behind 43 137 in this view. *AT8733*

Tinsley depot, in Sheffield, was home to many of the Class 45 locomotives in their later years, and a number of them were given unofficial names while there. 45 013 became 'Wyvern', and although it is not carrying the name in this view at Bristol Parkway on 18th February 1985, it has acquired a non-standard livery variation, with white lining around the grilles and windscreens, and along the upper bodyside. As a member of sub-class 45/0, this locomotive was equipped with steam heating only. Given the obvious leak between the second and third coaches, one wonders just how effective this was for the passengers on this Temple Meads to York service, on what was obviously a very cold day! *AT8755*

1985 marked the Great Western Railway's 150th anniversary, and a number of commemorative 'GWR 150' events were held during the year. Class 121 single unit 55020 and Class 117 unit B430 were both painted into Western Region lined Chocolate and Cream livery, complete with Lion and Wheel roundels. The latter set is seen here near Portbury on 25th May 1985, working one of the special services from Temple Meads to Portishead as part of the celebrations. A number of steam-hauled workings ran as well, and a run-round loop was laid at Portishead to cater for these. The track in this view appears relatively new, with concrete sleepers on fresh ballast, but whether this was done specifically for the GWR 150 events is not clear. *AT8958*

On 30th June 1985, F&W Railtours ran the marathon 'Severncider 2' tour, departing Cardiff Central at 05.15 and finally reaching Plymouth at 00.31 the following morning. It ran via Bristol, Worcester, Birmingham, Gloucester, Chepstow and Exeter, reversing many times, and taking in a number of little used and freight only lines en route. Motive power was provided variously by locomotives 08 836, 20 022, 20 115, 31 447, 37 215 and 47 538. In mid-morning, the second of these - 20 022 - brings up the rear of the train as it passes Victoria Park on the leg from Temple Meads to Wapping Wharf; 37 215 provided power at the front. An eastbound HST passes on the adjacent up main line. *AT9206*

Another view of the 'Severncider 2' railtour on 30th June 1985, this time at Hallen Marsh junction, with locomotive 31 447 in charge. From here, the Henbury loop line - which can just be seen to the right of the rear of the train - runs east to Filton, where it connects with the main line west of Bristol Parkway station. It was opened in 1910 to provide a more direct route to Avonmouth docks than those via Clifton or Pilning, and originally there were five intermediate stations and halts. Passenger services ceased in 1964, but the line remains in use for freight workings. The signal box here was closed and the semaphore signals removed in January 1988, with control of the area passing to St Andrews junction signal box, a little way to the south. *AT9214*

On 13th July 1985, Class 45 locomotives 45 130 and 45 036 run light past Dr Day's junction towards Filton Bank in company with an unidentified Class 47. This junction, named after Dr William Edward Day, a 19th century medical practitioner who lived nearby, forms the northern point of a triangle which includes Bristol East junction, near the end of Temple Meads station, and North Somerset junction, on the line towards Bath. At the date of this picture, both 45s were moving towards the end of their working lives, 45 036 being withdrawn just under a year later, on 11th May 1986, with 45 130 following on 10th May 1987. *AT9286*

The Class 116 three-coach units were built by BR's Derby works, with some 320 vehicles entering service during 1957 and 1958. They were the first of the 'high density' designs, virtually identical to the subsequent Classes 117 and 118, both of which were planned as 'follow-on' orders for Derby, but were put out to contractors due to changing priorities at the BR works. In January 1985, Tyseley set TS 611 received an unusual livery variation, with the grey upper body band extended around the vehicle ends to meet the black windscreen surrounds. This treatment is clearly visible in this view at Temple Meads on 7th September 1985, as the set departs with a summer Saturday extra from Birmingham to Weston-super-Mare. Also visible in this shot are a Class 08 shunter, and an HST in platform three. *AT9770*

The Class 20 locomotives represented the culmination of a number of single cab designs ordered under the Modernisation Plan pilot scheme during the 1950s. Construction was shared between English Electric and Robert Stephenson and Hawthorn Ltd, who together turned out 228 locomotives between 1957 and 1968. They fell into the type 1 bracket, with a power output of 1,000 hp and a Bo-Bo wheel arrangement. Intended primarily for light freight duties, they had no train heating equipment, although they were deployed on some passenger workings - particularly specials and charters - during the summer months. By the mid-1980s, a number of them had received the Railfreight sector grey livery, with red solebar and wrap around yellow ends, and locomotives 20 090 and 20 104 looked smart in these colours when caught by the camera at Hallen Marsh junction on 9th September 1985. *AT9785*

On 10th September 1985, Class 45 locomotive 45 103 crosses to the down loop at Stoke Gifford with a train of loaded ARC stone hoppers. This locomotive was a member of sub-class 45/1, totalling 50 machines which had electric train heating generators installed between 1973 and 1975, in place of their original steam heating boilers. This reflected the requirements of the later Mark 2 passenger coaches built from around 1970 onwards, which had electric heating and air-conditioning. However, 45 103 clearly had no need of this equipment on this particular working! *AT9788*

Although regular passenger services over the Henbury loop line ceased in 1964, North Filton platform, just to the west of Filton West junction, continued to be served by two trains a day until 9th May 1986. These were operated for the benefit of staff working at the aerodrome, and ran out from Bristol in the morning, and back in the afternoon. On 24th April 1986, just over a fortnight before final closure, Class 119 unit B591 awaits departure time at North Filton with the return working to Bristol. This station may yet see trains again under Phase 2 of the Metro West proposals, which envisage restoration of passenger services as far as a new station at Henbury. *AT10281*

On 19th June 1986, Class 47 locomotive 47 515 drifts down Filton Bank at Lockleaze with a train of British Army Land Rovers, trailers, and excavators. This locomotive had been wearing the 'large logo' livery for less than a year when this photograph was taken, and was to be repainted again, into 'InterCity' colours, before the end of August. On 25th September, it was named 'Night Mail' at Derby station by Bill Cockburn, Managing Director of Royal Mail Letters, as part of the relaunch of the TPO service. The relief lines at this location, taken out of use in 1984, had been removed completely by the date of this photograph. *AT10561*

The oil crisis of the early 1970s resulted in a significant increase in coal traffic on the BR network, and this created potential motive power problems, with much of the existing diesel fleet being of mixed traffic type, or due for retirement in the medium term. The solution was provided by the Class 56, a new 3,250 hp Co-Co locomotive, which entered service between 1977 and 1984. The order for these went to the Brush Group, with construction of 30 machines subcontracted to a Romanian company, Electroputere, and the remaining 105 to British Rail Engineering Ltd (BREL) at Doncaster and Crewe. They were allocated to the Eastern and London Midland regions, where they handled coal traffic, and to the Western Region for iron ore and aggregate workings. One of the latter is seen passing the long-closed Badminton station on 16th April 1987, behind locomotive 56 031, *Merehead*. *AT11624*

In advance of the 'GWR 150' celebrations, Class 50 locomotive 50 007 was repainted in Great Western lined Brunswick green livery in February 1984, and renamed *Sir Edward Elgar* in place of its original name, *Hercules*. The new cast brass nameplates were unveiled by Simon Rattle, conductor of the City of Birmingham Symphony Orchestra, in a ceremony at Paddington station on 25th April 1984. Neither the 'mock' livery (which none of the Class had ever worn), nor the break with the 'Warship' naming tradition, was universally popular with enthusiasts, but there is no denying that the locomotive looked very smart. It seems slightly out of place in this early evening view at Lockleaze on 16th May 1987, hauling a nondescript parcels train up Filton Bank. *AT11830*

Class 121 single car W55026, also carrying set number B126, passes St Andrews junction signal box and level crossing, just north of Avonmouth, with a service from Severn Beach to Bristol on 29th May 1987. For a few months during the previous year, this vehicle carried the Highland Rail 'Stag' logo on each end, very curious given that it was allocated to Bath Road depot at the time! The signal box here remains in use at the time of writing, though now with a panel controlling the line between Avonmouth and Henbury on the line to Filton. When photographed, the nameplate had been painted out for some reason. *AT12000*

Under the 1980s sectorisation programme, passenger services were split between InterCity, Network SouthEast, and Regional Railways, although a number of sub-sectors and 'brands' existed within each of these. Passenger services in Scotland were operated by Regional Railways, but were given their own distinct identity as 'Scotrail' from September 1983. A number of liveries were used by the sector, with some locomotives and hauled coaching stock carrying a modified version of the InterCity Executive scheme - the red stripe replaced by saltire blue, and 'ScotRail' branding in place of 'InterCity'. Class 47 locomotive 47 461, *Charles Rennie Mackintosh*, was a rare sight on two counts when photographed at Temple Meads working a service to Weston-super-Mare on 11th June 1987; first, because it was the only member of the 47/4 sub-class to wear these colours, and second, because it was an awfully long way from its home depot at Inverness! *AT12051*

The ability of multiple-units to work together depended on the compatibility of their electrical, control and braking systems. This was indicated by a system of coloured symbols painted near the jumper connections, such as a red triangle, white circle, or blue square. The majority of first-generation DMUs used the 'standard' blue square system, and so most classes could interwork. This provided a high degree of flexibility, as seen in this view of Class 108 driving trailer standard (DTS) W54207 leading a Class 122 single car near Lawrence Hill on 31st July 1987. The DTS had a gangway connection at its inner end, but this would have been locked out of use on this occasion as the single cars were not gangwayed. W54207 had been transferred from Hull to Bath Road only a few weeks before this photograph was taken, and still carried West Yorkshire PTE 'MetroTrain' branding. *AT12421*

Class 108 set B972 stands at Avonmouth with a train for Bristol Temple Meads on 4th August 1987. The Class 108s were built as two-, three-, and four-coach units by Derby works, some 333 vehicles being turned out between 1958 and 1961. They were of lightweight, largely aluminium construction, the motor vehicles weighing just 28 tons and the trailers 21 tons. Internal arrangements were high density, with two-plus-two seating in first class and two-plus-three in standard (which had replaced 'second' as a designation from May 1987). Set B972 had been formed at Bath Road only a few months before this photograph was taken, pairing Driving Motor Brake Standard (DMBS) M53627 with Driving Trailer Standard (DTS) E54210. These vehicles had previously been allocated to Allerton (Liverpool) and Hull respectively, and the DTS had started life as a composite but had had its first class accommodation downgraded. *AT12466*

On 6th August 1987, Class 31 locomotive 31 401 rolls down Filton Bank at Narroways with WR Inspection Saloon KDW 150266 in tow. Historically these vehicles - often referred to as General Manager's Saloons - allowed the directors and managers of the former railway companies to inspect their 'empires' from the large windows in each end of the coach. In BR days their deployment tended to be more practical, enabling engineers to examine infrastructure, or traincrew to learn new routes. Like many such saloons, KDW 150266 was rebuilt from a former catering vehicle, in this case a Collett designed composite restaurant car built at Swindon in 1925. It was converted to its later role in 1961, and subsequently spent a number of years in blue/grey livery before receiving chocolate and cream colours in time for the GWR 150 celebrations in 1985. *AT12537*

The particular working here is not recorded, but it looks as though an HST may have been in trouble! Class 56 locomotive 56 043, in Railfreight grey livery, hauls HST power car 43 012 northwards past Narroways Hill junction on 6th August 1987. The vehicle in between - a former Mark 1 open first - is a 'barrier vehicle', required because HST power cars had fixed-head buckeye couplers, and so could not attach directly to a locomotive with screw-link couplings. The line to Avonmouth and Severn Beach diverges here, just behind the train. *AT12536*

While passenger traffic diminished at night, the railway network remained busy with freight and mail. At just after 20.26 on 16th November 1988, Class 50 locomotive 50 015, *Valiant*, stands at the head of a westbound Travelling Post Office (TPO) service at Temple Meads' platform eight. From 1986, which marked the 50th anniversary of the publicity film, 'Night Mail', TPO vehicles were painted in the Post Office corporate style of red livery with yellow lining, and 'Royal Mail Letters' in yellow script, as seen on the first three vehicles here. The livery was to undergo a further minor change in 1990, the yellow lettering replaced with 'Royal Mail Travelling Post Office' in white italics, which remained until the operation ceased in 2004. *AT14880*

While the 'Pacer' units introduced from 1984 marked the initial steps towards replacement of the first-generation DMUs, a different solution was required for longer distance routes, where superior acceleration and greater passenger comfort were priorities. In response to a fairly broad technical specification, prototypes were built by BREL and Metro-Cammell, and these were developed into what became known as the 'Sprinter' family of units, comprising Classes 150, 153, 155, 156, 158 and 159. Although there were many detail differences, all had hydraulic transmissions, and all classes could interwork. Forty-two Class 155 units were built by British Leyland during 1987/8, each comprising two coaches seating 160 passengers in a two-plus-two layout. Only seven remain in their original formation; the remainder were converted to form Class 153 single cars in the early 1990s. On 16th November 1988, unit 155 325 stands at Temple Meads, sporting Regional Railways livery and 'Sprinter' branding. *AT14882*

Class 31 locomotive 31 430, *Sister Dora*, rests at Bath Road depot on 28th January 1989. Sister Dora was a 19th century Church of England nun and nurse, Dorothy Wyndlow Pattison, who worked in Walsall hospital. She cared for thousands of smallpox victims during the epidemic of 1875, and was especially remembered for her work with LNWR railwaymen who had suffered industrial accidents. Her funeral in 1878 was attended by a number of drivers, guards and porters in full uniform. The name *Sister Dora* was previously carried by an LNWR Waterloo Class 2-4-0 locomotive number 2158, and was applied to 31 430 at Bescot Yard on 9th October 1988. The locomotive has been preserved, and at the time of writing is based at the Spa Valley Railway in Kent. *AT14980*

Within the 'Sprinter' family of second-generation DMUs there were a number of sub-groups, Classes 153, 155 and 156 being designated 'Super Sprinters' (although only Class 156 carried this branding), while 158 and 159 - with 90 mph capability - were 'Express Sprinters'. The 114 sets of Class 156 were built by Metro-Cammell between 1987 and 1989, and shared many common features with Class 155. These included the power plant - a Cummins NT855R5 diesel engine under each coach, driving one bogie through a Voith T211r hydraulic transmission - together with the 23 metre coach length with single leaf sliding plug doors at vehicle ends, and a two-plus-two seating layout. Seating capacity, at 163 per unit, was marginally higher. On 11th February 1989, unit 156 448 leads an unidentified sister northbound past Dr Day's junction - the 'Super Sprinter' branding is visible to the left of the BR logo. *AT14994*

Members of Class 20 were the first locomotives to be sold to private operators for continued use on the BR network, with six machines transferred to Hunslet-Barclay for contract hire work in 1989. The locomotives involved - numbers 20 041/60/83/101/219/225 - were reclassified as 20/9, and renumbered as 20 901 to 906. Later sales saw Direct Rail Services (DRS) acquire fifteen Class 20/3 locomotives - their fleet ultimately including the Hunslet-Barclay machines - while other private operators also took on more of the 20s for Channel Tunnel construction work. Wearing its Hunslet-Barclay colours - which appear to be a variation of the Railfreight sector scheme - locomotive 20 904 is seen at the head of a weedkilling train at Ashton Exchange sidings on 11th April 1989. *AT15331*

The TOPS Class 97 was reserved for departmental locomotives used for special or engineering duties, and therefore included examples of several different classes grouped together. Four Class 47s - numbers 472, 480, 545 and 561 - were reclassified as 97s in 1988, and deployed on various testing activities for the Railway Technical Centre in Derby. As well as acquiring its new number in September 1988, 97 561 was also repainted in maroon livery, and on 23rd May 1989 was named *Midland Counties Railway 150, 1839-1989* in a ceremony at Derby station, commemorating the 150th anniversary of that company. A week later, on 30th May, it worked the 'Avonian' railtour from Derby to Bristol Temple Meads and return, and is seen here looking resplendent in Bath Road depot during the layover. The reclassification was short-lived however, with the locomotive renumbered as 47 973 just six weeks later, on 15th July. *AT15627*

The attractive countryside south of Wickwar tunnel is the setting for this view of Class 47 locomotive 47 525, hauling a Liverpool to Plymouth service on 20th June 1989. Wickwar, on the line between Gloucester and Bristol, was served by a station just north of the tunnel, but this closed in 1965 and the buildings have since been demolished. Entering service as D1108 on 28th January 1967, 47 525 was among the last of the 47s off the production line, with just eight delivered that year, and the final example following in 1968. As a member of sub-class 47/4, it was fitted with an electric train heating supply, essential for the air-conditioned stock in this consist The advance of new liveries is also apparent here, with the locomotive and seven of the nine coaches wearing InterCity colours. *AT15862*

The first of the production 'Sprinter' types, the Class 150, is represented here by unit 150 270, departing from Yate with a southbound service on 15th July 1989. These units were built by BREL between 1984 and 1987, and employed the suburban version of the Mark 3 bodyshell also used for several electric classes, with sliding doors at the one third/two thirds positions, and seating in a two-plus-three layout. Two sub-classes were built - 50 units of Class 150/1, which were very similar to the prototypes, and were only gangwayed within each set, and 85 units of Class 150/2, which had end gangways allowing access between sets. Engines and transmissions were identical to those on the later Class 155 and 156 units. Yate station had reopened just two months before this photograph was taken, on 11th May, having been closed to passengers since January 1965. *AT15948*

One of the most striking of the new liveries to appear during the 1980s was the grey, red, white and blue scheme developed for Network SouthEast, the branding adopted by the London and South East Sector from 1986. On 22nd July 1989, Class 47 locomotive 47 583, *County of Hertfordshire*, sports the early version of these colours as it passes Yate with the Saturdays only 06.50 Rose Grove (Burnley) to Paignton 'InterCity Holidaymaker' service - a change of scene from its weekday Oxford and Newbury commuter runs. A modified version of the livery began to appear at around this time, using a slightly darker shade of blue, and dispensing with the 'upsweep' of the grey, red and white stripes at the locomotive ends. The freight only line to the quarry at Tytherington can be seen curving away to the left of the locomotive. *AT15969*

Having operated as a single unit from its formation in 1982, 1987 saw the Railfreight sector divided up into six sub-sectors, each covering specific types of traffic. The sub-sectors were Coal, Construction, Distribution, General, Metals and Petroleum. At the same time, a new two-tone livery started to be applied to locomotives, and logos were developed for each sub-sector, these designed to be striking and clearly visible, even when less than clean! On 4th August 1989, Class 37 locomotive 37 063 passes Narroways Hill junction, wearing the new livery and the logo of Railfreight Distribution, the sub-sector tasked with handling non-trainload - or mixed - freight, as well as container traffic. The assortment of wagons in tow certainly appears in line with this allocation. The locomotive has split marker lights and end gangway doors, which mark it out as one of the first 119 of the Class to enter service. *AT16154*

A striking night-time view on Christmas Day 1989, showing a line-up of HSTs in the sidings at St Philips Marsh depot. Although difficult to see because of the reflected floodlights, power car 43 018, at far left, is wearing the later 'Swallow' InterCity livery, introduced from May 1987. As well as the swallow logo and new italic serif typeface, this scheme saw the yellow area cut back to cover just the vehicle end, with the lower red and grey bands extended all the way forward. St Phillips Marsh, on the Temple Meads avoiding line, was opened as a dedicated HST depot in 1976, taking the name of the original 1910 steam shed further west which had closed in 1964, and incorporating the 1959 Marsh Junction DMU depot. *AT16770*

With HSTs working the majority of InterCity services to Bristol, the South West, and South Wales, 28 of the Class 50 locomotives were eventually allocated to Network SouthEast, and all of these - except the celebrity green 50 007 - were repainted into the sector's colours. Many of them were deployed on Waterloo to Exeter services, work for which they were not entirely suited, with ten intermediate stops in just under 89 miles west of Salisbury, and reliability suffered as time went on. 50 032, *Courageous*, looks in a rather sorry state when captured by the camera at Bath Road depot on 22nd July 1990. It was withdrawn just under three months later, on 15th October, and scrapped in March the following year. *AT17597*

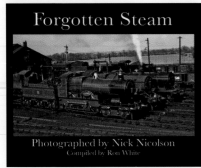

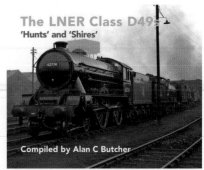

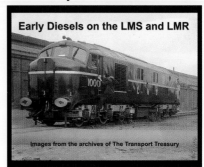